OCTAVE
and his
VIOLIN

Written and illustrated by
Gérard Moncomble

Assisted by
Jean-François Saint-Jean

To my little musicians

FINDING OUT ABOUT INSTRUMENTS

foulsham educational

To Jean-Luc Siret and
Daniel Delfour, instrument makers,
to Stéphane Muller, bow-maker,
my orchestrated thanks.

Gérard Moncomble

Design (Cover and Contents):
Jean-Louis COUTURIER
Lay out: Monique DIDIER

Printed in Czechoslovakia.

ISBN 0-572-01967-1

This anglicised edition copyright © 1994 W. Foulsham & Co. Ltd.
Original copyright © Bordas, Paris

All rights reserved

The Copyright Act prohibits (subject to certain very limited exceptions) the making of copies of any copyright work or of a substantial part of such a work, including the making of copies by photocopying or similar process. Written permission to make a copy or copies must therefore normally be obtained from the publisher in advance. It is advisable also to consult the publisher if in any doubt as to the legality of any copying which is to be undertaken.

foulsham
Yeovil Road, Slough, Berkshire SL1 4JH

Down the road, there is an extraordinary shop.

Where they sell strange, black cases.

The violin's identity card

Distinguishing marks: never without a bow.
Date of birth: about 1520.
Place of birth: Brescia and Cremona in Italy.
Length: 60 centimetres.
Weight: 400 grams.
Basic materials: wood, gut, aluminium and silver thread, steel.

Short arms, short violin
The weight and size of a violin and its bow vary according to the age of the player: teaching violins for children may measure as little as 40 centimetres.

They must all be great travellers.

I can spend hours looking in the shop window.

I have always been mad about boats.

and that of its bow

Distinguishing marks: never without a violin.
Date of birth: about 1520.
Place of birth: Brescia and Cremona in Italy.
Length: 75 centimetres.
Weight: about 60 grams.
Basic materials: wood (ebony, pernambuco), horse-hair, mother-of-pearl, silver thread, leather.

Zoo

A humped back like
A zebu
A pouched tum like
A kangeroo
No arms or legs like
A boa
A neck like
A giraffe ending in
A head with 4 ears
And 4 hairs clipped
in a big comb!!
My violin's
My little zoo

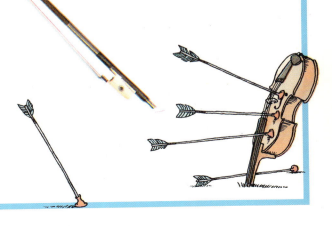

That is my favourite, the shiny, honey-coloured one.

If only I could be her captain!

A violin is ...

Sensitive to changes of temperature.

Portable You can take it anywhere.

Alive wood can change shape

We would sail the seas.

Together we would face storms and hurricanes,

stopping off for a break on an exotic beach.

... but it is not

An ornament
It is not to hang on a wall, it is to play.

Dangerous
Except in films.

A robot which plays by itself.

*Brown, brown, my violin,
All brown like crusty bread.*

*When I stroke
Your silken hair
Your words and songs
With me you share*

*Purr, purr under my chin,
Flutter and fly, like a butterfly.*

*Laughing, crying,
It's me inside,
A bag of tricks
Surprise, surprise*

*Brown, brown, my violin,
All brown like gingerbread.*

Today's the day: I'm going into Octave's cave!

There are boats in bits, all over the place,

The family album

The violin is part of the string family. Whatever their shape, they all work in the same way: the strings are stretched over a hollow box or a frame. You draw the bow over the strings or pluck them with your fingers.

The viola
Slightly larger than the violin. It has a lower pitch but also has four strings, C, G, D, A.

The 'cello
A sound like a human voice. It is played resting on its tail pin. C G D A (like the viola but an octave lower).

hanging up, in a row, waiting to travel.

That steamer is ready to take me round the world.

And with that sailing boat, I would fly like the wind.

The viols
A very old family of instruments with six or seven strings, rarely used today. They were played resting on the knees or between the legs.

THE ART OF BOWING
The sound obtained from bowing string instruments is similar to that of the human voice going from the highest pitch (the violin being the soprano) to the lowest, (double bass). With one difference, they do not have to pause for breath. The bow goes relentlessly on upwards and downwards: a bow stroke can keep the string sounding almost indefinitely. The strings may also be plucked: called 'pizzicato'.

Now, my granny She used to knit pullovers

The double bass
A descendant of the viols. It is the biggest and also the lowest pitched of all stringed instruments sometimes called Grandmother.
E, A, D, G.

The hold is ready to take in the bags, the barrels, the goods.

Now, if I close my eyes, I can smell the sea.

But as soon as I open them... Oh!

*F*amily album continued

THE ART OF PLUCKING
With your finger, your nail or a plectrum (a small bone or plastic strip). When you pluck the strings, you can either strike several together and produce a chord or just play a tune by plucking a single string at a time. Plucked stringed instruments are very popular as they have always been used to accompany songs and dances the world over.

The harp
Once over 3000 years ago, it was made of one single string stretched over a simple bow. Today it has 7 pedals and 476 strings.
Well done!

Hey! That's my boat! Someone is buying my boat!

I'll jump in before it takes off.

I'll never leave my little sailing boat, never!

The guitar
A very old instrument, too. But it is one of the most popular today. A round sound-hole and 6 strings: E, A, D, G, B, E.

What a family!

Lyre-guitar, Banjo, Pandurina, Cittern, Mandolin, Lute, Zither, Chinese guitar, Electric guitar, Balalaika, Hurdy Gurdy

Let's wait a minute. Not a sound.

I creep out of the box. Nobody in sight.

Aha, my boat! I can't believe it.

The guided tour of the violin

A wooden sculpture, entirely hand-made.

A giant sandwich with 70 fillings

Your turn
Try and find the names of all the parts

- a scroll
- b pegs
- c neck
- d finger board
- e ribs
- f bridge
- g tail piece strings G D A E
- h strings G D A E
- i f-holes
- j belly (top)
- k bass bar
- l back
- m soundpost
- n corner blocks

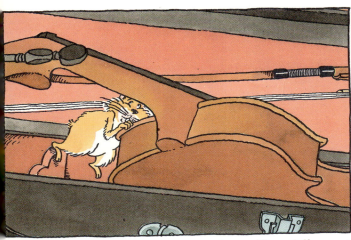
What a beauty! I am sure she will cut through the seas like a knife.

The hold is deep.

The ropes pulled tight.

ALL IN WOOD
The violin is made of wood, and wood alone. Ebony, maple, spruce, and pine – a whole forest.

A string charade

My first has 2 holes
My second a neck
My third a finger board
My fourth 4 pegs
And it all ends in a tail.

Who am I?

A horrible four-legged pneumatic kingfisher.

Of course not, silly,
My name is Violin

IN GUT AND METAL
The strings used to be made out of sheep gut. Then they were covered with silver and copper thread. Nowadays they can also be made of metal which gives a stronger sound. The violinist is free to choose. Simple gut strings are still used by early music groups seeking to reproduce the sweeter sound of a bygone age. The instruments are then played with the type of bow used in the 17th or 18th century.

The mast is slender but strong.

Right! Let's have a go.

Now, since we have not yet reached the sea.

The guided tour of the bow

It was originally made of a strand of hair stretched over a simple piece of wood. But, very rapidly the bow became the slender stick we know today, which is supple, yet tough, strong, yet sensitive and which has become as important as the violin itself.

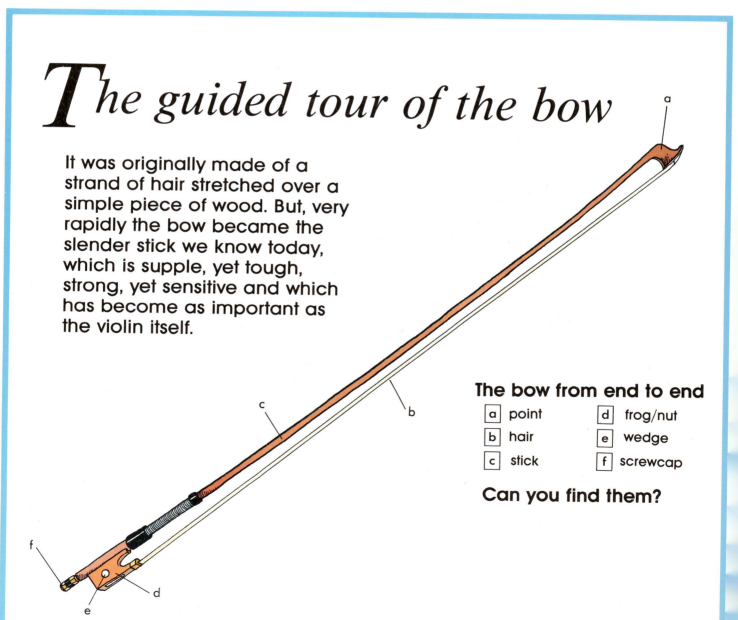

The bow from end to end
- a point
- b hair
- c stick
- d frog/nut
- e wedge
- f screwcap

Can you find them?

You will have your maiden voyage in the bubble bath.

Later, you'll see, we'll go to the ends of the earth.

Everything is ship shape.

THE GLOWING STICK

The stick is made of *pernambuco*, a very rare wood, the colour of glowing embers. It is so red, it was once used to colour fruit juice. It is found in Brazil which owes its name to this ember-coloured wood *(pao brasil)*. Another wood was once used, the *speckled mimosa*, also called *snake wood*. But what about the 150 strands which make up the hair of the bow? They come from the horse's tail. It is a real zoo we have here!

A strand of hair under a magnifying glass

Each hair is covered with scales just like a tortoise. However, to make sure it adheres to the strings strongly enough, each one is coated with a pine resin called 'rosin'.

The bow changes shape

Over the years, the bow has undergone a strange transformation: it originally resembled in its convex form, the weapon of the same name, but gradually it was made longer and the curve became concave. So the modern bow is in fact facing in the opposite direction to its ancestor.

Suddenly the lighthouse shines out.

Oh dear, here comes the keeper! I'll have to abandon ship.

"But that's my violin!"

How does the violin work?

Stroked by the hair of the bow, the strings vibrate...

This vibration passes through the bridge... which vibrates very rapidly from one foot to the other like a dancer.

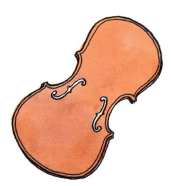

the belly
made of soft fir wood so the sound comes through easily.

the soundpost
a small piece of pine wood, wedged between the top and the back. It enables the sound to pass from one to the other.

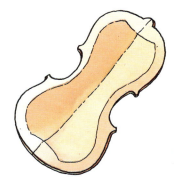

and the back
This is in maple, a hard wood which deflects the sound.

The vibration gets stronger and stronger and comes out through the two f-shaped holes in the top.

"What are you playing at, sonny?"

"I only wanted to go on a voyage."

"Listen to me then. This is how I travel."

The sound is low if the string is thick,
high if it is thin.
But it is also modified by the right hand on the finger board and
by the left hand using the bow.

THE SOUND IS

LOW

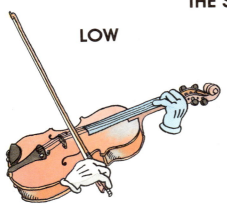

if the string is long

HIGH

if it is shortened

LOUD

if the bow plays near the bridge

SOFT

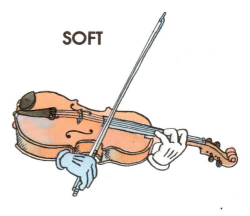

if it plays near the finger board. An even softer sound can be obtained by placing a mute on the bridge.

"Close your eyes... Now you are travelling without moving."

"So you aren't likely to be seasick."

"Let me tell you captain, people have been travelling like this for years."

The violin has a long history

The idea of drawing the bow across the strings, instead of plucking them may have come from Asia. Legend has it that Ravana, King of Ceylon, (Sri Lanka) invented the first bowed instrument 5000 years ago. In fact, nobody knows how far back bowed instruments go. In Europe, the bow has had a great success story. Starting with the rebec and continuing with the vielles, used extensively in the 14th century. After that came the viols and then the violins. For a long time, these two instruments were rivals but the power and brilliance of the violin made it the king of the strings and the sweeter bass viols are rarely seen today.

The Rebec
Descendant of the arab rabab, which was a popular instrument in the Middle Ages, especially among the wandering players and minstrels.

The vielles
Used by the troubadours for entertainment and dancing at court in the Middle Ages. They were held on the shoulder, against the chest or on the knees and played either with a bow or with the fingers.

"In the olden days you travelled as the fancy took you."

"Yes, well I prefer boats, so there!"

"Right, shipmate, we are going to travel in music."

The lyra
Seven strings, with two curiously placed next to the neck. It dates from the 15th century and comes from Italy. You can recognise it as the ancestor of the violin by its arched back, its sides carved out in a C form and its sound post.

The bow was a bit behind
The bow has changed too. As each new instrument was invented, the bow had to be adapted, but at the time of the invention of the the violin, it was not considered important. It only adopted its present form about 1770.

The violin of the Great Makers
Who among these famous Italians invented it? Andrea Amati? Giovan Giacobo dalla Corna? Zanetto da Montechiavo? Nobody knows! But here it is and it has hardly changed since 1500.

"This is the place we want."

"A violin for Octave? That's just up my street."

"Now, you must make sure it is water tight."

How the violin is made

The preparation
Once the maker has drawn the top and back with the help of a template, he cuts them out. Then the two pieces are hollowed out with a large round-bladed chisel, called a gouge. After that he files them down with a little plane. Finally the edges are whittled away with a small knife.

The mystery of the violin
Over the last 450 years, the violin has hardly changed its shape from that created by the great Italian instrument makers, like Amati, Guarnerius and Stradivarius in their workshops in Cremona. However, in 1830, it was slightly modified to accomodate new compositions. In Japan, one of Stradivarius' violins has been analysed by a computer and an identical copy made, except for the sound. The secret of the old violin has not yet been discovered.

The neck and the scroll
Carved out of a simple piece of wood, they emerge from the maker's hands in a scrolled form resembling a snail shell.

You cannot hurry wood
Wood freshly cut is damp and full of sap. It has to be left to dry for 5 years. Then it has to mature a long, long time. The instrument-maker is a patient fellow.

"I have a surprise for you, Captain Octave."

"What you'd call a surprise pack, ha ha..."

"But that might sink!" "Yes, but it should sing!"

Putting it all together

The ribs made by the instrument maker are curved with a hot iron and then joined to the plates using wooden blocks as shown here. All this is stuck together with a special product made from bone, rabbit skin and horse hoof. Then he adds the neck and scroll piece.

An old recipe for varnish

4 oz white amber
1 oz pearl mastic
1 oz copal and live gum
Dissolve these in 1 pound of wine spirit in a tightly closed glass recipient over warm embers or in the sunshine to obtain a pure white varnish.
Freely translated from "Traité des vernis" chez Laurent d'Houry, Paris, 1723

Varnishing

Each maker prepares his own varnish and keeps the recipe secret. He spreads it on with a brush and leaves it to dry. This operation is repeated about 10 times before he gives it a final polish. All that remains is to fit the finger-board, the pegs, the tailpiece, the strings, the bridge and the sound post. The job will have taken 200 hours.

"Look what I've made"

The bow maker

He, too, is something of a magician. Stripped from a block of pernambuco these sticks are made to dance on the strings of a violin. The bow maker's work is just as important as that of the instrument maker.

Hmph! We're in for a choppy time with this one.

Well, anyway, let's try.

"Now, for your first lesson."

Some funny ones!

Some violins are really comical. Ever since it existed and especially in the 19th century, people have tried to improve the quality of this instrument. Inventors have tried changing everything: the shape (like the one where the sound came out of a bell like a trumpet) the size, and the materials used: silver, leather, brass, plexiglass, and, wait for it, papier-maché.

Yes, well I tried chewing gum but it didn't work!

The kit
This was a violin small enough to fit into your pocket. Dancing masters used to find it very handy.

"First of all, you place your cheek so."

"Then you take the end bit of the end..."

"and you ... Octave! Are you listening?"

"OCTAVE!!"

Francis Chanot's violin
Halfway between the guitar and the violin. A strange mixture.

Felix Savart's violin
Rather like a pair of bellows in shape. Flat, with straight sound holes. But, unfortunately no instrument-maker would take it on.

Instrument making in the year 2000
And today, research is still going on:
into new materials (carbon)
into new shapes (the violin without corners and all in curves)
into new sounds (the electrified violin, which has a classic shape, and the electric violin, which is as flat as a pancake as it has no resonance chamber.)

"What did I tell you? It has sunk!"

"Octave, you are stubborn, but so am I."

"Plonk! Down into the hold with you!"

The violin can be found everywhere

Chamber music
Playing with friends. Here you see a quartet: first and second violins, a viola and a 'cello

The soloist
Skilled with the bow

"Not simple, the musical sa..."

"I am taking you to see other people who go travelling."

"My dear friends, may I introduce you to Captain Octave, my pocket violinist. He is coming on board."

Old Philibert Jambe de Fer was talking nonsense. In the beginning, the violin was considered mainly as a street instrument. People found it noisy and jangling, but just good enough for dancing to. The only qualities people found in it were that it was both easy to tune and to carry. In 1556, the composer Philibert Jambe de Fer, scornfully described it as "fine for the common folk to dance to." Viols were found to be sweeter in tone. And yet, today, with its immense repertory, the violin is one of the stars of the orchestra: right next to the soloist, there are thirty or more violinists. In fact, we are inundated with them!

Jazz
Just like the double bass, the violin has rhythm in its blood. Played on its own (as here) or amplified electronically.

And so, since then, I've been sawing away.

Sometimes with her...

Sometimes with him.

Everywhere

The violin travels all over the world.
It has always loyally served folk music.
In Central Europe, following the gypsy tradition. In Nordic countries where we find the Norwegian *fiolin* so like the Scottish and Irish instruments, all descendants of the very old Celtic *crwth*. In North America, it is the Cajun violin that gets everyone dancing and it is the same story in Peru, Mexico, Greece....
In the street, or in the concert hall, in dances and parties the violin calls the tune.

The gypsy violin
The bow becomes a real acrobat, jumping, bouncing, fluttering like a bird. An amazing feat.

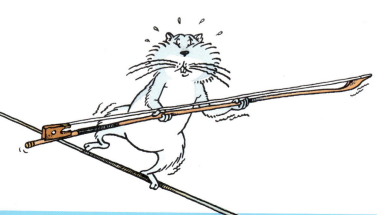

They have even made me Knight of the four strings.

You don't hear much of me during the concert, of course.

So I play my solos to those who do listen.

**The Symphony Orchestra
An ocean of bows
heaving up and down**

An ideal hiding place for Octave Hood!

Now, I no longer mix up fiddling and sailing.

I am called Captain Bowstring.

My friends take me all over the world with them.

The violinist and his violin

"A man travelling with his voice in his instrument case. The violinist, more than all other musicians must learn to catch the movement of sound (...)"

Freely translated from Yehudi Menuhin "Voyage Inacheve" 1976 Ed. du Seuil.

The left hand
A real virtuoso. It knows every inch of the neck which is just as well as there is nothing to tell you where the notes are.

The right hand
Its job is not just pushing and pulling the bow: it plays all sorts of figures with its skippings and bouncings, harmonics and martellatos, ricochets, staccatos and legatos. An acrobatic duo.

The chin and the collar bone.
That is where the violin snuggles up for a cuddle. The chinrest was invented about a century ago, before that, the violin rested on the shoulder.

The score
How on earth do you turn the page to find your notes when you are holding a bow? Fortunately the violinist usually knows his music by heart.

Tuning
Before the violin is played, the pegs are tuned so that the four strings play G D A E

The wood of the violin
It inevitably becomes dusty and sticky because of the rosin and needs to be carefully cleaned with a chamois leather. In a hot climate, you may have to push a tube of water down through the sound holes to prevent the wood drying out. And you need to watch a violin constantly: little worms love violin for supper!

The violin case
A real treasure chest. Two bows, just in case, rosin, a tuning fork, a chamois leather, a hygrometer to measure the humidity of the air, and, often the musician's personal bits and bobs.

Today is the day my dream came true. I am off on a cruise on the biggest violin in the world. See you. . . .

PICTURE CREDITS

Photography by Jean PORTES and Francoise VERGNES :
• **p. 4** : *Violin* • **p. 5** : *Bow* • **p. 8** : *Viola : Cello* • **p. 11** : *Guitar* • **p. 20** : *Preparation : Neck and Scroll* • **p. 21** : *Putting together : Varnishing*

• **p. 3** : Ph. M. Didier/©Photeb • **p. 9** : *Viola da Gamba and Treble Viol* Ph. © J.P. Dumontier/Artephot *Double bass*, Ph. Jeanbor © Photeb • **p. 10** : *Harp* by Naderman Pere, end XVIIIth C., Musée Instrumental, Paris, Ph. Publimages © Photeb • **p. 18** : *Rebec*, Sculpture on the doorway of Saint Marie cathedral at Glozon, 12th C, Ph ©J. P. Dumontier/ Artephot, *Vielle*, Musée Instrumental, Paris, Ph. Publimages © Photeb • **p. 19** : *Lyra*, Kunsthistorisches Museum, Vienne, Ph © Kunsthistorisches Museum, Vienne; *Violin* made by Andrea Amati in 1566, Musée Civique, Cremona, Ph. © Museum • **p. 22** Kit, Stradivarius 1717, Cremona, Musée Instrumental, Paris, Ph. Publimages/© Photeb • **p. 23** : *F. Chands' violin,* Paris, 1818. Musée Instrumental, Paris, Ph. Publimages/© Photeb, *F. Savart's violin*, Paris, 1819, Musée instrumental, Paris, Ph. Publimages © Photeb **p. 24** *Y. Menuhin*, Ph. © G. Neuvecelle: *Quartet : Via Nova*, Ph © G. Neuvecelle • **p. 25** : *Stephane Grapelli*, Ph. © G. Neuvecelle • **p. 26** : *Myrko Layosh, gypsy violinist*, Ph. © G. Neuvecelle • **p. 27** *Orchestra conducted by C. Peita*, Ph. © G. Neuvecelle.

English translation Moira Allouche with technical advice from Nicholas Burton-Page, Professor of Early Music at the National Conservatoire of the Region of Aubervilliers-La Courneuve.